Bead Knitted Pendant Bags Etc. 2

THE LS52, LS53, LS64, & LS66 PURSE FRAMES REFERENCED AND PICTURED IN THIS BOOK HAVE BEEN REPLACED BY THE BL52, BL64, & BL66 GOLD & SILVER PURSE FRAMES ALSO MARKETED AS PF52, PF53, PF64 & PF66

Comprehensive Instructions and Patterns for Two Pendant Bags and One Handbag

Theresa Williams

Photo Gallery Highlights

Front Cover: Clockwise from top: *Sundance* pendant bag (multicolored tiger-eye beads with beaded necklace), *Storybook Charm* handbag (wine colored beads with ribbon work embellishment and beaded fabric handle), and *Simply Speaking* bracelet/pendant bag (blue/green beads with ribbon embellishment and bracelet).

Front Inside Cover: *Sundance* pendant bag

Back Inside Cover: *Storybook Charm* handbag.

Back Cover: *Simply Speaking* bracelet/pendant bag.

Copyright © 1996 by BagLady Press, L.L.C.
First Printing August, 1996
Published by BagLady Press, L.L.C.
P.O. Box 2409
Evergreen, CO 80437-2409
U.S.A.

This booklet was written to provide clear instruction and to inspire creativity in the making of bead knitted bags. Every effort has been made to ensure that the contents of this booklet are accurate and complete. However, due to differing materials, procedures, conditions, tools and individual skills, the publisher cannot be responsible for any injuries, losses, and other damages which may result from the use of the information contained in this booklet.

ISBN 1-887989-05-6

Introduction

Sometimes in life one thing leads to another and sometimes things lead to beads. Sally Warner says, "We are tricked by a phenomenon of time: hours and days pass slowly, but years pass quickly." Bead knitting fosters an awareness of the present moment, overcoming this phenomenon of time. Each stitch counts, each stitch will never happen again, each stitch is perfect as it is, and all stitches taken together create something that is greater than the sum of the individual parts. The creator and work become one - little effort is expended, the work flows together effortlessly and harmoniously.

Bead Knitted Pendant Bags Etc. 2 brings you an arpeggio in beads, played note by beaded note. Next to each other, this lovely trio of bags builds to a resounding chord topped with the sparkling grace of silk ribbon embellishments and charms. A twist, a gleam, a textured finish to make a three-part harmony wherever you go. Enjoy each and every moment making these bags.

Theresa Williams
The BagLady™

Table of Contents

Table of Figures

Knit, Slip, Knit

Knit 1, slip 1,
this is relaxing fun.
Knit 1, slip 2,
my life is like a zoo.
Knit 2, slip 3,
this is a luxury.
Knit 3, slip 4,
uh oh,
someone's knocking at the door.
Knit 4, slip 5,
go 'way,
uhhhh,
my husband has the hives.
Knit 5, slip 6,
... right smack dab....
in the middle of a stitch.
Knit 4, slip 8,
I guess you just won't wait.
Knit, slip, knit, slip,
stop rushing me,
slip 8.

Theresa Williams
The BagLady™

1. BASICS

1.1 Skills

Knitting: You must know or learn the following knitting skills:
Casting On
Basic Knit Stitch
Increasing a Stitch
Binding Off

Sewing: Basic hand and machine sewing skills are useful for assembling these bags.

Ribbon Work: Basic ribbon work techniques are used to embellish these bags. The ribbon work involves traditional techniques of folding or gathering ribbon in order to manipulate it into various flower and leaf shapes.

Other: Reach into your personal skill bag and consider applying your other needlework and beading skills to these bags.

1.2 Tools and Materials

Beading Needles and Thread: Medium sized beading needles and nylon beading thread is useful. I use size 12 beading needles and size D beading thread to make the beaded fringe.

Beads: Purchase the number of hanks of seed beads (see Appendix A, Definitions) specified for each design. These patterns assume that there are 12 strands of beads on each hank purchased. If the hanks have fewer than 12 strands, you may need to purchase an additional hank.

See Section 1.4 for a fast way to transfer a strand of beads to the perle cotton. Most bead shops stock hanks of seed beads. The most readily available seed beads are glass and are made in Czechoslovakia. Take note of the various finishes that are available in these seed beads such as iris, matte, silver lined, and several others. (Be advised that if you wish to use loose beads, i.e. those not strung onto string, you will need to string these beads onto the perle cotton one-by-one in preparation for knitting).

1

These patterns are designed for size 11 seed beads. Bead size impacts the shape and size of the finished project. If you experiment with other sizes, keep in mind that the higher the number of bead, the smaller the bead.

Corks: Get yourself a couple of small corks, pop gun size. I push a cork onto one end of each of my knitting needles for larger projects (you are working on double pointed needles here). The purpose for this is to prevent the knitting from sliding off the back side of the needle.

Embellishments: I stockpile beads, charms, buttons, and ribbons. When I see something I like, I buy it. I worked with the following embellishments in these designs.

Charms - Charms are everywhere, in bead stores, fabric stores, needlework shops, craft stores, and your jewelry box.

Beads - In addition to seed beads, other types of beads can be incorporated into ribbon work, or strung from the bottom of the bag.

Wire Ribbon - Ombre wire ribbon is exciting. I purchase 2-3 yards of a color at a time. Green is useful - buy plenty for leaves.

Fabric: For appearance and for the purpose of keeping with tradition, I use silk fabrics with drape for the lining. Faille or satin are a more practical option for wear and tear. Satin, however, can ravel while you work with it - which can be a frustration.

Knitting Thread: These designs are knitted with #8 Perle Cotton. I am familiar with the following three brands:

Anchor® & DMC® - These brands come in a wide range of colors and are easy to find. It is easy to transfer the beads onto these threads without trouble.

Finca® - This brand comes in a smaller range of colors. However, Finca® produces some colors that DMC® and Anchor® do not such as two shades of turquoise. Some knitting and weaving shops carry this brand. Finca® seems to be a somewhat thicker thread. It takes a bit of extra effort to transfer the beads onto this thread yet I really like the finished results.

Other Knitting Threads: If you get curious, experiment with other types of threads. There are several silk threads out on the market that look like fun. Just remember that if you want your bag to come out

2

close to the size specified in the pattern, you will have to gauge your work accordingly.

Knitting Needles: Size 0000 (U.S.), or 1.25mm (metric) double pointed knitting needles.

Purse Frames: All designs require metal purse frames.

- *Sundance* uses the 2.1 inch curved LACIS frame LS 64 (gold or nickel plate),

- *Storybook Charm* uses the 3.5 inch curved LACIS frame LS 52 (gold) or LS 53 (silver), and

- *Simply Speaking* uses the 2.5 inch square LACIS frame LS 66 (gold or nickel plate).

If your local retailer does not carry these frames, contact one of the suppliers listed in Appendix B.

Stabilizer: Stabilize the bag with a non-fusible medium weight interfacing when applying ribbon work.

Frame Backing: Metal is naturally hard and sometimes sharp. Bead knitting is naturally soft and delicate. Before I put anything sharp together with something delicate I carefully examine the situation. Prior to sewing my bags (particularly the larger bags) onto a metal purse frame, I examine the frame for sharp edges or burrs. If there is anything that I wouldn't want to have against my knitted piece, I make a backing and place it between the frame and the knitted piece. If you decide to back the frame, consider using Ultrasuede®, it works well.

1.3 ẞints Before Starting

Construction Scratch Sheets: Construction scratch sheets are provided, in the back of this booklet to assist in the knitting of the bags, pages CSS-1 through CSS-5.

Knitting: The bead knitting technique used for these bags is straightforward, fluid, and extremely fast. Use whatever knitting technique you know and are comfortable with. Each bag is knitted flat, using two knitting needles.

The beads are slid (the knitting term is "slipped" see Appendix A, Definitions) into place between stitches at designated intervals. The knitted stitch on either side of the beads locks them in place. As you

3

slide the beads into place between stitches and knit them in - be sure your stitch locks into place securely enough so that the beads stay put. Take special care when slipping 7-8 beads at a time. You may want to slow your knitting down at this point. Keep a firm tension throughout the knitting process - but there is no need to go overboard.

The beads appear on the underside of each row as they are knitted in. The significance of this point is that the beads will show on both sides of your knitted bag. The process of increasing or decreasing the number of beads between the stitches is what forms the shape of the bag.

Once you move farther along into the knitting pattern and as the knitted piece becomes longer, you may want to place a pillow in your lap and rest your arms and the knitted piece on it while knitting. Larger pieces can get quite heavy and this weight can tire your forearms. Take care of your arms in this respect.

Please note the following about the instructional style used in this booklet:

1. In Subsections 2.1.3 and 2.2.3, when a pair of asterisks (*) bracket an instruction, the instructions between the asterisks are to be repeated when you see the words "repeat * from row __".

2. In Subsections 2.1.3, 2.2.3 and 2.3.3, the format "(knit__, slip__beads; __times)" is used. In this case, the instructions preceding the semicolon are to be performed the number of times specified after the semicolon. For example the instruction "(knit 3, slip 5 beads; 3 times)" means to perform the instruction, "knit 3, slip 5 beads", 3 times.

Color and Texture: As you select the beads and perle cotton, look for contrast in color and texture. Even a slight contrast will produce a more striking finished project. If both the color and texture of the beads and perle cotton match perfectly, there will be little notice of the fact that your work is beaded. Examine the photographs with this in mind.

Keep in mind that the color of your perle cotton may alter the color of the beads. Taken to the extreme, if you string white beads onto a black thread, the color of the beads will be altered. In this case they will appear somewhat grayed.

Gauge: While the gauge for bead knitting is primarily determined by the bead size the following two points are important:

1. It is important that you like the feel or drape of your piece. This is determined by the tension.

2. For each of these designs, it is important that your knitting is gauged to ensure the bag and frame fit each other. The fit doesn't have to be exact but the bag must be large enough to drape nicely from the frame.

For these reasons I suggest that you make a sample swatch prior to venturing into a design. This piece will be a 18 stitch by 40 row swatch. Load a couple of strands of beads onto the perle cotton following the directions in Section 1.4, and knit the gauge as follows:

Cast on 18 stitches.

Rows 1-6   Knit 18.

Rows 7-36   Knit 4, slip 2 beads, (knit 2, slip 2 beads; 5 times), knit 4.

Rows 37-40   Knit 18.

Bind Off

Starting with and including the first column of "slip 2 beads", measure 1 inch across the middle of your swatch. There should be 8 stitches and 9 beads per inch. Options for adjusting the gauge follow:

1. To make the gauge bigger:

   a)   Use one larger size needle-size 000,

   b)   Cast on and place extra stitches at each end of the knitting,

   c)   Use size 10 seed beads,

   d)   Knit looser, or

   e)   Some combination of the above.

2. To make the gauge smaller:

   a)   Use a smaller size needle-size 00000,

   b)   Reduce the number of cast on stitches, or

   c)   Knit tighter.

1.4   Transferring the Beads to the Perle Cotton

You must transfer a portion of the seed beads onto the perle cotton prior to beginning the knitting. These bags are large enough that it is not practical to transfer all of the strands of beads to the perle cotton at one time. I transfer 5-7 strands at a time depending upon where I am in the process of sliding beads. I tend to transfer more strands when sliding 6-8 beads at a time and fewer strands when sliding 1-5 beads. When you have knitted in all or nearly all of the beads you transferred onto the perle cotton, complete the row that you are working on, break the thread and add more beads. **DO NOT** try to add beads in the middle of a row. The work looks messy if the thread is broken in the middle of a row.

The following is the fastest and easiest way I know of to transfer a full strand of beads to the perle cotton all at once.

1. Do one of the following:

   a) Break one end of one strand of beads from your hank. The rest of the hank is still intact and attached, or

   b) Break one end of one strand of beads from your hank. Secure the end by tying a large knot in the end. Cut the other end of the strand from the hank so that it is free.

2. Fold the thread you broke over onto itself forming a loop. Make an overhand knot to hold this loop in place(See Figure 1). If there isn't enough thread exposed to make the knot, remove a few beads until there is enough room. Basically, you will have made the seed bead strand into a "string needle" having an eye at one end and the straight of the needle being the portion of the strand holding the beads. This knot is small enough that the seed beads will slide over it.

3. Thread the free end of the perle cotton through the eye of the "string needle". Pull the perle cotton through the eye leaving a tail of at least 8 inches.

4. Carefully slide the beads over the knot and over onto the perle cotton. If a bead refuses to slide over onto the perle cotton - unthread the string needle, remove the naughty bead, and start the process again.

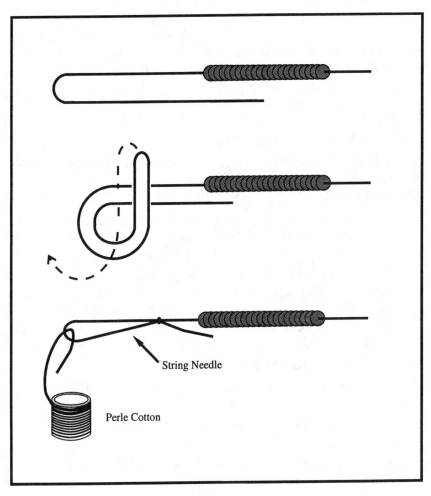

Figure 1
Making the String Needle

7

NOTE:

When transferring the beads to the perle cotton watch for irregular shaped or colored beads. Remove any beads that you would not want in your finished project at this time. Removal once you start knitting requires that you cut your strand of knitting at the end of a row, remove the unwanted bead, and begin knitting again. It is more convenient to catch any unwanted beads at this stage.

Lifesavers:

Dealing with Thick Bead Strand Thread:

Occasionally a hank of beads will be strung onto thicker thread. In this case you will need to take an additional step prior to transferring the beads as described above. Do one of the following:

1. Tie the strand of beads to size 80 or smaller sewing thread using a square knot. Transfer the beads from the strand onto the sewing thread. The beads will slide onto the sewing thread very easily. Then work as described in Step 2 above, or

2. Untwist the bead strand thread so that one ply of the strand is free. This is a little tricky and twirly but it can be done. Then make the string needle with this ply of the strand. Proceed with caution - this thread is not strong and it can break easily if you get rambunctious.

Unloading Beads from the Perle Cotton:

If the perle cotton knots as you knit, and there are beads threaded in front of the knot, you can rectify the situation as follows:

1. Starting about 6 inches from the free end, untwist the plys of the perle cotton.

2. Insert size 80 or smaller sewing thread in between the plys of the perle cotton. Pull the sewing thread through about 6 inches. Twist the plys back up.

3. Gently slide the beads onto the spool of sewing thread.

4. Make a string needle as described above, remove the knot from the perle cotton, and reload the beads.

1.5 Metric Conversions

This booklet uses the inches and yards unit of measure. Use the following formulas to convert to the metric equivalents:

1 inch = 2.5 centimeters

1 yard = .9 meters

To convert inches to centimeters, multiply the inches by 2.5. To convert yards to meters, multiply the yards by .9.

"At a certain point, you have to go to the edge of the cliff and jump __ put your ideas into a form, share that form with others." **Meredith Monk**

2. Bag-by-Bag Instructions

2.1 Sundance

Nurturer, replenisher, purveyor of warmth, light and life! Knit a bit of the sun's sweet light. Guaranteed to brighten your outlook.

> *"The artistic process is more than a collection of crafted things; it is more than the process of creating those things. It is a chance to encounter dimensions of our inner being and to discover deep, rewarding patterns of meaning."*

Peter London

2.1.1 *Materials*

1 hank of size 11 seed beads.

1 full ball of #8 perle cotton.

LACIS frame model LS 64 (gold or nickel plate).

Chain, beads, or fabric for handle of purse frame.

Charms, if desired.

2.1.2 *Overview*

This bag measures approximately 2 inches wide across the top, $3\frac{3}{4}$ inches wide across the widest part of the bottom, and 3 inches long (including the frame). Across the top portion of the bag there are 8 vertical sections of beads which increases to 12 vertical sections of beads about one-third down from the top of the bag. The bag consists of a total of 124 rows of knitting.

2.1.3 *Detailed Knitting Instructions*

Use the construction scratch sheets on pages CSS 4 & 5 for this bag.

Cast on 26 stitches.

Rows 1-6	Knit 26.
Rows 7-10	Knit 6, (slip 1 bead, knit 2; 7 times), slip 1 bead,

	knit 6.
Rows 11-20	Knit 6, (slip 2 beads, knit 2; 7 times), slip 2 beads, knit 6.
Rows 21-22	Knit 4, slip 1 bead, (knit 2, slip 3 beads; 8 times), knit 2, slip 1 bead, knit 4.
Rows 23-24	Knit 4, slip 2 beads, (knit 2, slip 3 beads; 8 times), knit 2, slip 2 beads, knit 4.
Rows 25-26	Knit 2, slip 1 bead, (knit 2, slip 3 beads; 10 times), knit 2, slip 1 bead, knit 2.
Rows 27-28	Knit 2, slip 2 beads, (knit 2, slip 3 beads; 10 times), knit 2, slip 2 beads, knit 2.
Rows 29-34	Knit 2, slip 2 beads, (knit 2, slip 4 beads; 10 times), knit 2, slip 2 beads, knit 2.
Rows 35-38	Knit 2, slip 2 beads, (knit 2, slip 5 beads; 10 times), knit 2, slip 2 beads, knit 2.
Row 39	Knit 2, slip 2 beads, (knit 2, slip 5 beads; 10 times), * knit 1, slip stitch 1, wrap the slipped stitch, slip wrapped stitch back onto the original needle, **TURN YOUR WORK AND GO TO THE NEXT ROW NOW.** (See Section 1.3 for definition of * and Appendix A for a discussion of short rows and wrapping a stitch)
Row 40	Knit 1, slip 5 beads, (knit 2, slip 5 beads; 9 times), repeat * from row 39.
Row 41	Knit 1, slip 5 beads, (knit 2, slip 5 beads; 8 times), repeat * from row 39.
Row 42	Knit 1, slip 5 beads, (knit 2, slip 5 beads; 7 times), repeat * from row 39.
Row 43	Knit 1, slip 5 beads, (knit 2, slip 5 beads; 6 times), repeat * from row 39.
Row 44	Knit 1, slip 5 beads, (knit 2, slip 5 beads; 5 times), repeat * from row 39.
Row 45	Knit 1, slip 5 beads, (knit 2, slip 5 beads; 4 times), repeat * from row 39.

Row 46	Knit 1, slip 5 beads, (knit 2, slip 5 beads; 3 times), repeat * from row 39.
Row 47	Knit 1, slip 5 beads, (knit 2, slip 5 beads; 2 times), repeat * from row 39.
Row 48	Knit 1, slip 5 beads, knit 2, slip 5 beads, repeat * from row 39.
Row 49	Knit 1, slip 5 beads, (knit 2, slip 5 beads; 5 times), knit 2, slip 2 beads, knit 2.
Row 50	Knit 2, slip 2 beads, (knit 2, slip 5 beads; 10 times), knit 2, slip 2 beads, knit 2.
Rows 51-86	Repeat rows 39 through 50, 3 times. This takes you through row 86.
Rows 87-90	Knit 2, slip 2 beads, (knit 2, slip 5 beads; 10 times), knit 2, slip 2 beads, knit 2.
Rows 91-96	Knit 2, slip 2 beads, (knit 2, slip 4 beads; 10 times), knit 2, slip 2 beads, knit 2.
Rows 97-98	Knit 2, slip 2 beads, (knit 2, slip 3 beads; 10 times), knit 2, slip 2 beads, knit 2.
Rows 99-100	Knit 2, slip 1 bead, (knit 2, slip 3 beads; 10 times), knit 2, slip 1 bead, knit 2.
Rows 101-102	Knit 4, slip 2 beads, (knit 2, slip 3 beads; 8 times), knit 2, slip 2 beads, knit 4.
Rows 103-104	Knit 4, slip 1 bead, (knit 2, slip 3 beads; 8 times), knit 2, slip 1 bead, knit 4.
Rows 105-114	Knit 6, (slip 2 beads, knit 2; 7 times), slip 2 beads, knit 6.
Rows 115-118	Knit 6, (slip 1 bead, knit 2; 7 times), slip 1 bead, knit 6.
Rows 119-124	Knit 26.

Bind off.

2.1.4 Assembly

See Chapter 4, Section 4.1 to determine if you will block the piece.

1. Fold the main piece, first and last rows together. Sew the bag to the frame following the instructions in Chapter 4, Section 4.3, "Sewing the Bag to the Frame".
2. Using perle cotton sew the side seams up by hand. Weave any loose ends into the side seams.
3. For the necklace use chain or string beads together and attach to the purse frame.
4. Embellish the bag with beads or charms, if desired.

2.2 Storybook Charm

> *"When you work you are a flute through whose heart the whispering of the hours turns to music.*
>
> *...And what is it to work with love? It is to weave the cloth with threads drawn from your heart, even as if your beloved were to wear that cloth..."*

Kahlil Gibran, The Prophet

2.2.1 *Materials*

5 hanks of size 11 seed beads.

1 full ball of #8 perle cotton.

16 inch x 10 inch piece of fabric for lining.

LACIS frame model LS 52 (gold) or LS 53 (silver).

$\frac{1}{2}$-1 yard of trim for inside edge of bag, optional.

Chain, beads, or fabric for handle of purse frame.

7 inches of $1\frac{1}{2}$ inch wide wired ombre ribbon for leaves ($3\frac{1}{2}$ inch length required for each leaf).

$1\frac{1}{2}$ yards of $\frac{1}{4}$ inch ribbon of your choice for Daisy (satin, rayon or silk).

$18\frac{1}{2}$ inches of 1 inch wide wired ombre ribbon for Azalea.

Charms, if desired.

2.2.2 *Overview*

This bag measures approximately $3\frac{1}{2}$ inches wide across the top, $7\frac{3}{4}$ inches wide across the bottom, and $6\frac{1}{4}$ inches deep (including the frame).

The front and back are knitted as one piece. Across the top portion of the bag there are 14 vertical sections of beads which increases to 16 vertical sections of beads about one-third down from the top of the bag. The two gussets are knitted separately and sewn into the sides of the bag to add depth and dimension to the overall design. The bag consists of 272 rows of knitting.

8 rows of plain knitting, followed by:

4 rows with one bead every 2 stitches,

20 rows with 2 beads every 2 stitches,

2 rows with a mix of 2 and 3 beads every 2 stitches,

2 rows with 3 beads every 2 stitches,

6 rows with 4 beads every 2 stitches,

12 rows with 5 beads every 2 stitches,

10 rows with 6 beads every 2 stitches,

40 rows with 7 beads every 2 stitches,

64 short rows with 7 beads every 2 stitches,

40 rows with 7 beads every 2 stitches,

10 rows with 6 beads every 2 stitches,

12 rows with 5 beads every 2 stitches,

6 rows with 4 beads every 2 stitches,

2 rows with a mix of 2 and 3 beads every 2 stitches,

2 rows with 3 beads every 2 stitches,

20 rows with 2 beads every 2 stitches,

4 rows with 1 bead every 2 stitches,

8 rows of plain knitting.

2.2.3 Detailed Knitting Instructions

Main Piece

Use the construction scratch sheets on pages CSS-2 &3.

Cast on 38 stitches.

Row 1-8   Knit 38.

Rows 9-12   Knit 6, (slip 1 bead, knit 2; 13 times), slip 1 bead,

	knit 6.
Rows 13-32	Knit 6, (slip 2 beads, knit 2; 13 times), slip 2 beads, knit 6.
Rows 33-34	Knit 4, slip 2 beads, knit 2, (slip 3 beads, knit 2; 14 times), slip 2 beads, knit 4.
Rows 35-36	Knit 4, (slip 3 beads, knit 2; 15 times), slip 3 beads, knit 4.
Rows 37-42	Knit 4, (slip 4 beads, knit 2; 15 times), slip 4 beads, knit 4.
Rows 43-54	Knit 4, (slip 5 beads, knit 2; 15 times), slip 5 beads, knit 4.
Rows 55-64	Knit 4, (slip 6 beads, knit 2; 15 times), slip 6 beads, knit 4.
Rows 65-104	Knit 4, (slip 7 beads, knit 2; 15 times), slip 7 beads, knit 4.
Row 105	Knit 4, (slip 7 beads, knit 2; 14 times), slip 7 beads, * knit 1, slip stitch 1, wrap the slipped stitch, slip wrapped stitch back onto the original needle, **TURN YOUR WORK AND GO TO THE NEXT ROW NOW.** (See Section 1.3 for definition of * and Appendix A for a discussion of short rows and wrapping a stitch)
Row 106	Knit 1, (slip 7 beads, knit 2; 13 times), slip 7 beads, repeat * from row 105
Row 107	Knit 1, (slip 7 beads, knit 2; 12 times), slip 7 beads, repeat * from row 105.
Row 108	Knit 1, (slip 7 beads, knit 2; 11 times), slip 7 beads, repeat * from row 105.
Row 109	Knit 1, (slip 7 beads, knit 2; 10 times), slip 7 beads, repeat * from row 105.
Row 110	Knit 1, (slip 7 beads, knit 2; 9 times), slip 7 beads, repeat * from row 105.
Row 111	Knit 1, (slip 7 beads, knit 2; 8 times), slip 7 beads, repeat * from row 105.

Row 112	Knit 1, (slip 7 beads, knit 2; 7 times), slip 7 beads, repeat * from row 105.
Row 113	Knit 1, (slip 7 beads, knit 2; 6 times), slip 7 beads, repeat * from row 105.
Row 114	Knit 1, (slip 7 beads, knit 2; 5 times), slip 7 beads, repeat * from row 105.
Row 115	Knit 1, (slip 7 beads, knit 2; 4 times), slip 7 beads, repeat * from row 105.
Row 116	Knit 1, (slip 7 beads, knit 2; 3 times), slip 7 beads, repeat * from row 105.
Row 117	Knit 1, (slip 7 beads, knit 2; 2 times), slip 7 beads, repeat * from row 105.
Row 118	Knit 1, slip 7 beads, knit 2, slip 7 beads, repeat * from row 105.
Row 119	Knit 1, (slip 7 beads, knit 2; 8 times), slip 7 beads, knit 4.
Row 120	Knit 4, (slip 7 beads, knit 2; 15 times), slip 7 beads, knit 4.
Rows 121-168	Repeat rows 105 - 120, 3 times, this takes you through row 168.
Rows 169-208	Knit 4, (slip 7 beads, knit 2; 15 times), slip 7 beads, knit 4.
Rows 209-218	Knit 4, (slip 6 beads, knit 2; 15 times), slip 6 beads, knit 4.
Rows 219-230	Knit 4, (slip 5 beads, knit 2; 15 times), slip 5 beads, knit 4.
Rows 231-236	Knit 4, (slip 4 beads, knit 2; 15 times), slip 4 beads, knit 4.
Rows 237-238	Knit 4, (slip 3 beads, knit 2; 15 times), slip 3 beads, knit 4.
Rows 239-240	Knit 4, slip 2 beads, knit 2, (slip 3 beads, knit 2; 14 times), slip 2 beads, knit 4.
Rows 241-260	Knit 6, (slip 2 beads, knit 2; 13 times), slip 2 beads, knit 6.

17

Rows 261-264	Knit 6, (slip 1 bead, knit 2; 13 times), slip 1 bead, knit 6.
Rows 265-272	Knit 38.

Bind Off.

Gussets: Knit two of these.

Cast on 6 stitches.

Rows 1-6	Knit 6.
Rows 7-12	Knit 2, slip 3 beads, knit 2, slip 3 beads, knit 2.
Rows 13-76	Knit 2, slip 4 beads, knit 2, slip 4 beads, knit 2.
Rows 77-82	Knit 2, slip 3 beads, knit 2, slip 3 beads, knit 2.
Rows 83-86	Knit 6.
Row 87	Knit 2 tog[1]; 3 times.
Rows 88	Knit 2 tog, knit 1.

Bind off.

2.2.4 *Assembly*

If blocking, refer to Chapter 4, Section 4.1.

1. See Chapter 4, Section 4.3, "Sewing the Bag to the Frame" to add a backing to the frame, if desired.

2. Fold the main piece, first and last rows together. Sew the bag to the frame following the instructions in Chapter 4, Section 4.3, "Sewing the Bag to the Frame". Do not sew the gussets until step 4.

3. Referring to the instructions in Chapter 3, "Ribbon Work Techniques" stabilize and embellish the bag as shown in Figure 8, page 26.

4. Starting at or just below each side hinge of the frame, sew the gussets into the sides of the bag.

5. Make and sew the lining in place following the instructions in Chapter 4, Section 4.2, "Making a Lining".

6. For the handle, use chain, make one from fabric, or string some beads together and attach to the purse frame. To make the fabric

---

[1] tog is the abbreviated knitting term for together

handle, cut a 2 inch wide by 26 inch long piece of fabric. Fold the fabric lengthwise, with right sides together, and sew a $\frac{1}{4}$ inch seam forming a tube. Turn the tube right side out. Thread the tube through one of the metal loops on the purse handle and bring the raw edges together. Twist the tube loosely upon itself and thread the raw edges through the other loop, and sew in place. Sew beads at random onto the handle.

2.3 Simply Speaking

"Everything should be made as simple as possible, but not simpler." **Albert Einstein**

This design is simple. Dress it up or down to take with you anywhere you go.

2.3.1 *Materials*

2 hanks of size 11 seed beads (if including fringe).

1 full ball of #8 perle cotton.

LACIS frame model LS 66 (gold or nickel plate).

Chain, beads, bangle bracelet, or fabric for purse frame handle.

8 inches of $1\frac{1}{2}$ inch wide wired ombre ribbon for Pansy.

6 inches of 1 inch to $1\frac{1}{2}$ inch wide wired ombre ribbon for leaves (3 inch length required for each leaf).

Charms, if desired.

2.3.2 *Overview*

This bag measures approximately $2\frac{1}{4}$ inches wide across the top, $3\frac{3}{4}$ inches wide across the bottom, and $3\frac{3}{4}$ inches deep (including the frame). The front and back are knitted as one piece. Across the top portion of the bag there are 7 vertical sections of beads which increases to 15 vertical sections of beads about one-third down from the top of the bag. The bag consists of 158 rows of knitting.

2.3.3 Detailed Knitting Instructions

Use the construction scratch sheet on page CSS-1 for this bag.

Cast on 28 stitches.

Row 1-6	Knit 28.
Rows 7-12	Knit 5, (slip 1 bead, knit 3; 6 times), slip 1 bead, knit 5.
Rows 13-17	Knit 5, (slip 2 beads, knit 3; 6 times), slip 2 beads, knit 5.
Row 18	Knit 3, knit 2 tog, (slip 2 beads, knit 2 tog, knit 1; 6 times), slip 2 beads, knit 3, knit 2 tog.
Rows 19-24	Knit 4, (slip 3 beads, knit 2; 6 times), slip 3 beads, knit 4.
Rows 25-32	Knit 4, (slip 4 beads, knit 2; 6 times), slip 4 beads, knit 4.
Rows 33-36	Knit 3, slip 2 beads, (knit 1, slip 4 beads, knit 1, slip 2 beads; 7 times), knit 3.
Rows 37-40	Knit 3, slip 3 beads, (knit 1, slip 4 beads, knit 1, slip 3 beads; 7 times), knit 3.
Rows 41-120	Knit 3, (slip 4 beads, knit 1; 14 times), slip 4 beads, knit 3.
Rows 121-124	Knit 3, slip 3 beads, (knit 1, slip 4 beads, knit 1, slip 3 beads; 7 times), knit 3.
Rows 125-128	Knit 3, slip 2 beads, (knit 1, slip 4 beads, knit 1, slip 2 beads; 7 times), knit 3.
Rows 129-136	Knit 4, (slip 4 beads, knit 2; 6 times), slip 4 beads, knit 4.
Rows 137-142	Knit 4, (slip 3 beads, knit 2; 6 times), slip 3 beads, knit 4.
Row 143	Knit 3, knit 1 and increase 1 into this stitch, (slip 2 beads, knit 1 and increase 1 into this stitch, knit 1; 6 times), slip 2 beads, knit 1, knit 1 and increase 1 into this stitch, knit 2.
Rows 144-148	Knit 5, (slip 2 beads, knit 3; 6 times), slip 2 beads,

knit 5.

| Rows 149-154 | Knit 5, (slip 1 bead, knit 3; 6 times), slip 1 bead, knit 5. |
| Rows 155-158 | Knit 28. |

Bind Off.

2.3.4 *Assembly*

1. Fold the main piece, first and last rows together. Sew the bag to the frame following the instructions in Chapter 4, Section 4.3, "Sewing the Bag to the Frame".

2. Referring to the instructions in Chapter 3, "Ribbon Work Techniques" stabilize and embellish the bag as shown in Figure 9, page 27.

3. Using perle cotton sew the side seams up by hand. Weave any loose ends into the side seams.

4. To finish with beaded fringe, see Chapter 4, Section 4.4, "Beaded Fringe". Embellish the bag with beads or charms, if desired.

"Intuition is the clear conception of the whole at once." **Johann Lavater**

3. Ribbon Work Techniques

"The work will teach you how to do it."

Estonian Proverb

Unless otherwise noted, embellish the bag prior to sewing the side seams or gussets. Stabilize the bag in preparation for ribbon work by pinning medium weight non-fusible interfacing to the wrong side of the bag.

The techniques used in these designs are described and illustrated below.

Simple Ribbon Leaf

Cut a 3 inch length of 1 to $1\frac{1}{2}$ inch wide ombre ribbon for *Simply Speaking* and a $3\frac{1}{2}$ inch length of $1\frac{1}{2}$ inch wide ombre ribbon for *Storybook Charm*. Fold each end at right angles toward the center of the ribbon. Baste along the widest edge of the ribbon with a thread knotted at one end. Gather by pulling the thread and secure in place.

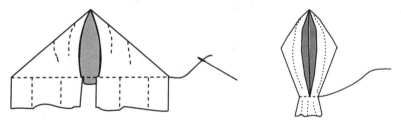

Figure 2
Simple Ribbon Leaf

Pansy

Cut an 8 inch length of $1\frac{1}{2}$ inch wide ombre ribbon. Run a gathering thread, $\frac{5}{8}$ inch from the edge, and stitch a point on the narrower side as shown in Figure 3. Gather the ribbon tightly, with the narrow part folding over the wider part as shown in Figure 4. Stitch the raw edges of the pansy "face" together using the gathering thread. Fold the remaining raw edges under and tack. Add beads to the center.

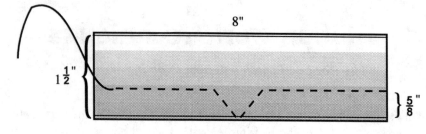

Figure 3
Pansy Cutting

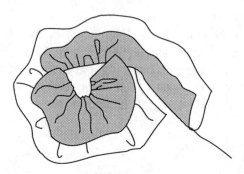

Figure 4
Pansy Gathering

Azalea

1. Cut one 11 inch length and one $7\frac{1}{2}$ inch length of 1 inch wide ombre wired ribbon. Remove wire from the darker edge. Beginning and ending $\frac{1}{4}$ inch from the ends, mark the 11 inch length at $3\frac{1}{2}$ inch intervals, as shown in Figure 5.

2. GATHER-STITCH each length of ribbon, following the dotted stitching line, making 3 SQUARED-OFF PETALS; see Figure 5. Pull the thread tightly to gather petals. Connect first and last petals, securing with stitches. Repeat with the $7\frac{1}{2}$ inch length, marking at $3\frac{1}{2}$ inch intervals (2 petals).

3. Sew beads in the center of the flower.

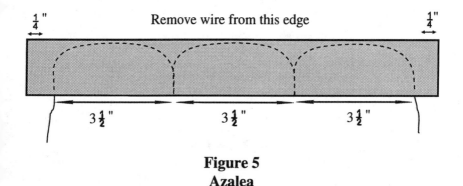

$\frac{1}{4}$ " $\frac{1}{4}$ "

$3\frac{1}{2}$ " $3\frac{1}{2}$ " $3\frac{1}{2}$ "

Figure 5
Azalea

Daisy

Cut 18 to 20, $2\frac{1}{2}$ inch lengths of $\frac{1}{4}$ inch wide ribbon of choice. Fold each length as shown in Figure 6. Stitch lengths together with a $\frac{5}{8}$ inch seam allowance, using the GATHERING STITCH as shown in Figure 7. Pull thread tightly to gather petals and secure with a knot. Trim seam allowance to $\frac{1}{4}$ inch. Stitch completed daisy flower to the bag as shown in Figure 8.

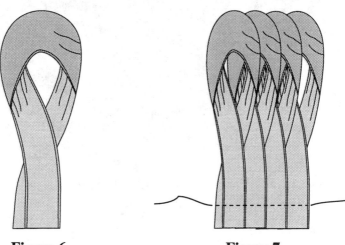

Figure 6   **Figure 7**
Daisy Petal   **Daisy Flower Assembly**

25

Azalea
1" Wire Ribbon

Simple Ribbon Leaf
$1\frac{1}{2}$" Wire Ribbon

Daisy
$\frac{1}{4}$" Ribbon
of Choice

Figure 8
Storybook Charm

26

Simple Ribbon Leaf
1" to 1½" Wire Ribbon

Pansy
1½" Wire Ribbon

Figure 9
Simply Speaking

4. Finishing Instructions

"An artist should never lose sight of the thing as a whole. He who puts too much into details will find that the thread which holds the whole thing together will break." **Frederic Chopin**

4.1 Blocking

If you think it is necessary to tidy up the shape of the knitted piece it can be done by blocking. If blocking the work, do it prior to applying the embellishments. Test the materials for colorfastness before jumping into this process. If you are confident about colorfastness, mist the piece with a spray bottle filled with cool water. The piece should be wet - but not soaking wet. Next lay the knitting out on a piece of foamboard, gently pull it into shape, and insert straight pins to keep it in place until it dries.

4.2 Making a Lining

1. Trace or make a photocopy of the finished bag. Trace the size of the finished bag and add $\frac{1}{2}$ inch around all sides. This allows a $\frac{1}{2}$ inch ease in the finished size of the lining and for a $\frac{1}{4}$ inch seam allowance. Slightly square off the tracing at the base of the frame to allow enough ease for opening and closing. It's important to have enough fullness here. If you are unsure of your tracing, cut a prototype out of muslin or other inexpensive fabric and do a test run.

2. Pin the lining in place along the inside edge of the frame. Fold the raw edges of the lining toward the wrong side of the fabric as you pin it in place. Stitch the lining in place by hand unless otherwise suggested. After sewing the lining into the bag, tack it down in a few places along the seamlines, as needed.

3. Add a touch of romance to the bag-a touch of hidden beauty-make it something special inside and out. Add a lovely braid, velvet ribbon, or beads along the inside edge of frame. I think that opening up a bag should be like entering a world of hidden treasures - a world of

possibilities. The bag should transcend a utilitarian purpose, making it a fine work of art.

4.3 Sewing the Bag to the Frame

If you are not backing the frame, go to Step 2.

1. The easiest way I know of to make a backing for a frame is to first make a pattern of the frame. I copy the frame, actually put it on the copy machine, and use the copy as the pattern. Cut the shape of the frame from the paper - this is your pattern. Lay the pattern on the Ultrasuede® or other fabric and cut it out slightly larger than the pattern, to allow for fitting. Lay the backing against the underside of the frame and tack it to the frame in a few places using invisible thread or other thread. You just need to tack it in place, because when you sew the bag to the frame, the backing then becomes fully sewn in place.

2. Center the top edge of one side of the bag to the inside of the frame. I suggest opening the frame as flat as it will go without breaking or stressing it. If necessary, use safety pins by inserting them through the holes of the frame for placement of the bag onto frame in about six places.

3. Using perle cotton, invisible thread, or other strong thread, and working from the center toward one side of the bag, sew the bag by hand to the frame. Use any stitch that gives you the look you want. Secure the thread at the base of the frame (by the hinge), take a couple of back stitches, and tie off. Repeat in a similar manner for each quarter of the top of the bag and frame, until the bag is fully sewn to the frame.

4.4 Beaded Fringe

Anchor some bead thread to the bottom corner of the inside of one seam of the bag. String 2 inches or so of beads on the thread at a time, bring the needle up through the bottom of the bag forming narrow loops and down again. Continue stringing beads in a similar manner across the bottom of the bag to the other side.

Appendix A

Definitions

<u>Hank of Beads</u>: A bundle of individual strands of strung beads.

<u>Slip Beads</u>: Slide the indicated number of seed beads into place against the previous knit stitch prior to knitting the next stitch.

<u>Slip Stitch</u>: Take one stitch off the left hand needle and put it on the right hand needle (without knitting it), if you are right handed. Reverse direction if you are left handed.

<u>Short Rows:</u> The short rows form the curved bottom on the *Sundance* and *Storybook Charm* bags. On these bags the short rows are rows 39-50 and 105-120 respectively, with each set performed a total of 4 times. Short rows are really just partial rows of knitting which shape or curve a section of your knitted piece. The resulting effect of the short rows is that one side or section has more rows than the other, with no stitches being decreased. The technique of the short rows is sometimes referred to as turning since the work is turned within a row. Figure 10 shows a conceptual set of short rows.

<u>Wrapping a Stitch</u>: When short rows are used in pieces such as these, you must make a smooth transition between the edge where one row is worked and the edge that has the extra row. This is done by "wrapping" a slipped stitch. Pull the perle cotton to the front of the knitting. Another way to look at it is to place the perle cotton between the slipped stitch and the needle holding the stitches to be knitted next. Figure 11 shows the three steps needed to wrap a stitch for the beaded bags.

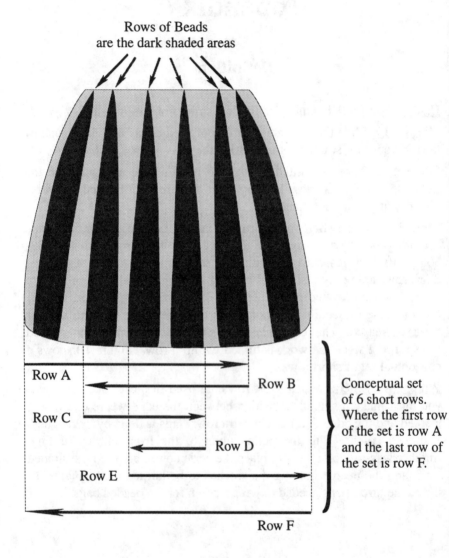

Rows of Beads
are the dark shaded areas

Row A

Row B

Row C

Row D

Row E

Row F

Conceptual set
of 6 short rows.
Where the first row
of the set is row A
and the last row of
the set is row F.

**Figure 10
Conceptual
Short Row Shaping**

1. To prevent holes in the piece and create a smooth transition, wrap a knit stitch as follows: With the yarn in back, slip the next stitch purlwise.

2. Move the yarn between the needles to the front of the work.

3. Slip the same stitch back to the left needle. Turn the work, bringing the yarn to the purl side between the needles. One stitch is wrapped.

Figure 11
Wrapping a Stitch

Source: <u>Vogue Knitting, The Ultimate Knitting Book</u>, 1989, Pantheon Books, New York, NY, The Butterick Company, Inc. Page 186. Reprinted by Permission.

Appendix B

Sources

In addition to your local bead, knitting, fabric, needlework, craft, and hobby stores, the following are also good sources for the materials needed to make these bags:

BagLady Press, L.L.C., P.O. Box 2409, Evergreen, CO 80437-2409. Books, metal purse frames and size 0000 knitting needles. Toll free order number (888) 2BAGLADY (222-4523). Denver metro area (303) 670-7105.

International Beadtrader, Inc., 3435 S. Broadway, Englewood, CO 80110. Full service bead supplier including seed beads, glass beads, stone beads, metal beads, findings, charms, cording, metal purse frames, and knitting needles. Cost of catalog is $5.00 which is refundable with the first order. (303) 781-8335 in the Denver metro area, all others (800) 805-2323.

LACIS, 3163 Adeline Street, Berkeley, CA 94703.
Specializes in fine beads, metal purse frames, materials, and needles for beadwork. Send $5.00 for complete catalog. (510) 843-7178.

Ornamental Resources, P. O. Box 3010, Idaho Springs, CO 80452.
Cost of catalog is $15 which includes updates for one year. Specializes in old and rare glass beads, pendants, and stones. They also carry the metal purse frames and 0000 knitting needles. (303) 279-2102 in the Denver metro area, all others (800) 876-6762.

Appendix C

References

Beadwork

The Basics of Bead Stringing, A Complete Illustrated Approach For Beginner and Advanced Designer, Mel Anderson; 1985, Borjay. A good resource for the basics of stringing beads and jewelry construction.

Bead Work, edited by Jules and Kaethe Kliot; 1984, Lacis Publications. Includes examples, patterns, and ideas for various beaded needlework.

Knitting

Mary Thomas's Knitting Book, Mary Thomas; 1938, Hodder & Stoughton, London, reprinted in 1985. Good basic instructions. (May have to be special ordered.)

Vogue Knitting, The Ultimate Knitting Book, Pantheon Books, 1989.

Knitting Made Easy, Coats & Clark, 1993. Good basic knitting booklet.

Ribbon Work and Silk Ribbon Embroidery

Gardening with Ribbons, Diane Herbort and Bonnie Benson, 1994, Quilter's Resources Inc. An excellent resource for ribbon work techniques and materials.

Elegant Stitches, An Illustrated Stitch Guide and Source Book of Inspiration, Judith Baker Montano, 1995, C&T Publishing. Comprehensive instructions and diagrams for ribbon embroidery stitches.

Appendix D

Care Guidelines

Washing: Prior to washing a bag, I strongly recommend that you prepare and wash a swatch made from the perle cotton, beads, and ribbon used on your finished piece. The swatch doesn't have to be a work of art - the object here is to test for colorfastness. If you are confident that the piece is colorfast, it is possible to wash the bag by hand. Gently swish it out in cool soapy (mild soap) water. Rinse the bag with cool water and lay it out flat to dry. Spot cleaning can work too.

Storage: When my bags are not is use, I wrap them in acid free tissue paper and store them in a plastic bag. Acid free paper prevents yellowing and aging.

Displaying: If you decide to display your bags, avoid displaying items in or near direct sunlight. Perle cotton, beads, and ribbon are all susceptible to fading from direct sunlight.

Use: Take a reasonable amount of care when using your bags. The major concern is for snagging or catching the bead knitting.

Construction Scratch Sheets

Simply Speaking

Row #'s	Count	Total Row Count
1-6		6
7-12		6
13-17		5
18		1
19-24		6
25-32		8
33-36		4
37-40		4
41-120		80
121-124		4
125-128		4
129-136		8
137-142		6
143		1
144-148		5
149-154		6
155-158		4

Start Date	Bead Color
Finish Date	Thread Brand
Bead Size	Thread Color

CSS-1

Construction Scratch Sheets

Storybook Charm

Row #'s	Count	Total Row Count
1-8		8
9-12		4
13-32		20
33-34		2
35-36		2
37-42		6
43-54		12
55-64		10
65-104		40
105		1
106		1
107		1
108		1
109		1
110		1
111		1
112		1
113		1
114		1
115		1
116		1
117		1
118		1

Construction Scratch Sheets
Storybook Charm
Continued

119		1
120		1
121-168		48
169-208		40
209-218		10
219-230		12
231-236		6
237-238		2
239-240		2
241-260		20
261-264		4
265-272		8

Gussets

Row #'s	Count Gusset 1	Count Gusset 2	Total Count
1-6			6
7-12			6
13-76			64
77-82			6
83-86			4
87			1
88			1

Start Date	Bead Color
Finish Date	Thread Brand
Bead Size	Thread Color

Construction Scratch Sheets
Sundance

Row #'s	Count	Total Row Count
1-6		6
7-10		4
11-20		10
21-22		2
23-24		2
25-26		2
27-28		2
29-34		6
35-38		4
39		1
40		1
41		1
42		1
43		1
44		1
45		1
46		1
47		1
48		1
49		1
50		1
51-86		36

Construction Scratch Sheets

Sundance
Continued

87-90		4
91-96		6
97-98		2
99-100		2
101-102		2
103-104		2
105-114		10
115-118		4
119-124		6

Start Date	Bead Color
Finish Date	Thread Brand
Bead Size	Thread Color

BagLady Press Information

BagLady Press, L.L.C. is dedicated to awakening, inspiring, and nourishing artistry and creativity at all levels. We believe in the tradition, spirit, and artistry of the past as the foundation for exploration and discovery in today's world.

As a purveyor of fine art and craft designs, our goal is to unleash your artistic and creative powers through publications that open doors to freedom of expression and innovation in the arts and crafts.

Any comments and/or suggestions can be sent to:

BagLady Press, L.L.C.
P. O. Box 2409
Evergreen, CO 80437-2409
U.S.A.

Tel: (303) 670-2177
Fax: (303) 670-2179
(email) baglady@baglady.com
World Wide Web Site http://www.baglady.com

Toll free order line: 1-888-2BAGLADY (222-4523). In the Denver metro area call (303) 670-7105 to order BagLady Press books, the metal purse frames used in our designs, and size 0000 (1.25mm) knitting needles.

Other Publications by BagLady Press, L.L.C.:

Bead Knitted Pendant Bags, ISBN 1-887989-03-X

Bead Knitted Handbags 1, ISBN 1-887989-01-3

Bead Knitted Handbags 2, ISBN 1-887989-02-1

Bead Knitted Pendant Bags Etc. 1, ISBN 1-887989-04-8

Bead Knitted Pendant Bags Etc. 3, ISBN 1-887989-06-4